Do Your Prayers Bounce Off the Ceiling?

Do Your Prayers Bounce Off the Ceiling?

Grant A. Worth

Deseret Book Company
Salt Lake City, Utah

No part of this book may be reproduced in any
form or by any means without permission in writing
from the publisher, Deseret Book Company,
P.O. Box 30178, Salt Lake City, Utah 84130

First printing January 1982
Second printing June 1983
Third printing March 1985

Library of Congress Cataloging in Publication Data

Worth, Grant A., 1943-
    Do your prayers bounce off the ceiling?

    Includes index.
    1. Prayer. 2. Spiritual life—Mormon authors.
I. Title.
BV215.W63   248.3′2   81-17411
ISBN 0-87747-895-3   AACR2

Contents

This book
is lovingly dedicated
to my mother,
Adrienne Worth

Preface

Early in my life, I experienced difficulty in consistently receiving and discerning answers to prayer. Frequently, when I had a difficult decision to make I would approach God humbly and sincerely and ask for his guidance. Yet, I would sometimes feel that perhaps the Lord was leaving me to make my own decisions.

I quickly learned how wrong I was. The Lord is always ready to provide his comforting guidance and help. He will not leave us alone. Later, I learned that my problem had been that I didn't know how to discern answers to prayer, even though I knew how to pray.

During the years I served as a bishop, I counseled with many people who had similar problems. In doing so, I learned of many factors that contribute to success with prayer. This book was written to share these principles with those who may be having the same difficulties I had.

I express my love and appreciation to all with whom I counseled over the years. I learned and grew through the spiritual experiences we shared. I especially appreciate my loving wife, who provided significant encouragement during the writing of this book.

1

Why Can't I Get an Answer?

Serving as a bishop I had many opportunities to counsel people who were struggling with prayer. I have struggled personally with prayer. It seems that the problems others have experienced are not unlike my own. Regardless of how many positive, spiritual experiences I have with prayer, it remains a difficult task to make prayer an effective form of spiritual communication every day of my life. I suspect that on some days we all feel that our prayers just don't seem to leave the room. They seem merely to bounce off the ceiling.

Much of our prayer is directed toward finding out the Lord's will in our behalf. We go to him for guidance on decisions we need to make. Yet, several people have told me that they aren't sure that they have ever really received an answer from God on a decision they have made. These have included a Primary president, a Sunday School president, a member of an elder's quorum presidency, and others in responsible Church positions. As these people seek divine guidance in staffing and leading their organizations, they experience frustration because they do not know with confidence that their decisions are inspired by their Father in Heaven. They want to hear God's answers to their prayers, but in many cases they feel they don't know how to obtain an answer.

This same frustration exists with many of us as we seek to know the Lord's will regarding our personal lives. Shall I take the new job? Shall we continue dating? Should I go on a mission? Shall we get married? Should we buy a new house? Is it time to get a new car? Can we afford this vacation trip? What should my career be? How should we discipline the children? The questions and decisions go on and on. Thus, the purpose of this book is to provide some guidelines for us to use in examining our own success, or lack of success, with prayer, and to provide help and encouragement for making prayer a more effective spiritual tool in our lives.

Basic Prayer Mechanics

This book does not emphasize the mechanics of prayer. I hope that you already have a good understanding of prayer and that, for you, prayer is a way of life. This book is for the person who already knows how to pray, who knows that prayers should be offered in secret, with a feeling of humility, in a kneeling position, vocally, often with fasting, and unceasingly. You have probably eliminated bad prayer habits, such as excessive repetition or allowing your mind to wander during prayer. You should recognize that you must have a sincere purpose and pray with real intent. It is essential to acknowledge God's hand in all things and to offer gratitude continually for the outpouring of his blessings.

These basic elements of prayer are essential. If you have not mastered them, I earnestly suggest that you commit yourself to these principles, developing good prayer habits as you read this book.

Is More Required?

Even with good prayer habits, many have difficulty knowing when they have or have not received an answer from God. Many yearn for spiritual manifestations which they feel they never receive. Many have exercised sincere prayer and feel that they practice the basic prayer mechanics, but have still experienced difficulty. Some who have been successful and have received unmistakable answers to prayers on one occasion have encountered difficulty on their next attempt.

Do we need to do more than follow the good prayer habits identified above? What are some of the barriers in receiving answers to our prayers? What can we do differently to have greater success? In order to offer some possible answers to questions like these and to provide encouragement and hope I offer this book. It is my sincere prayer that it will help you grow closer to your Father in Heaven.

2

I've Tried That.
It Still Doesn't Work!

Each time I have had the opportunity to counsel those who are having difficulty receiving answers to prayer, I have reviewed with them the basic prayer principles that generally lead to success. It is not infrequent to find someone for whom it is a new idea that, when possible, they should pray vocally, even in private. I have occasionally talked with individuals who routinely say their prayers lying on their back in bed and who seldom, if ever, kneel in prayer. I believe the basic prayer mechanics are essential, and I am aware of many people who had been experiencing difficulty but solved their problems by following these basic principles.

However, in most cases, after I review with people the basic principles of prayer, they say, "I've tried all that, but I still can't get an answer."

What's Your Problem?

As I have counseled with others, and as I have reviewed my own personal successes and failures, I have

4

identified several possible reasons for experiencing difficulty with prayer. Some find that the reason for their problem is simply that they fail to study issues out in their own mind, make a decision, and then offer this decision to God for his approval. Instead, they ask God to make the decision for them.

Others seem to ask the wrong questions altogether. They may be, so to speak, asking whether to choose option X or option Y, when in reality they should be considering option Z.

We often fail to have effective communication with God because we don't know how to listen to or recognize God's response. What does a "burning in the bosom" feel like? Is it always powerful? What is a "stupor of thought"?

Many of us experience difficulty because we don't feel worthy to receive an answer. This feeling is a tool of Satan to keep us from experiencing success with prayer.

Sometimes our faith is weak and we don't know how to strengthen it. We occasionally approach prayer with an attitude of, "I won't get an answer. I never do!" And sure enough, we don't!

Occasionally we are afraid of a particular response to a prayer. Sometimes our selfish interests become a barrier to learning what the will of the Lord truly is. No matter how sincere we are in wanting to do the Lord's will, we must always be careful to distinguish between his will and our own.

There are those who have suggested to me that "God doesn't really want us bothering him with all our decisions. Isn't it likely that he wants us to make our own decisions and stand on our own two feet?" All too often this attitude becomes a barrier to effective divine communication, and occasionally it promotes rationalization and decisions leading toward selfish interests.

It is my prayer that each of us may learn to more effectively communicate with our Father in Heaven and that we may be prepared to receive his guidance at all times. As we conquer problems and develop good prayer habits and practices in our lives, we will one day be able to communicate with our Father in Heaven as easily and as effectively as we might do with our own earthly fathers.

3

Petition or Decision?

I believe the major difficulty in receiving answers to prayers is associated with making decisions. I have seldom heard individuals complain about not receiving health or wisdom in answer to prayer. In almost all cases, the complaints about not receiving answers to prayers have come from those who are trying to make a decision and want to make a correct decision. They want to follow a correct path but feel that they need God's help.

I remember when a certain young man was sitting across from me. He was a good husband and a father of two children. He was dedicated to living the gospel and was a fine individual. He came to me, his bishop, for counsel about starting his own business. He was skilled in the service he had to offer and was confident that he could develop and maintain a dedicated clientele.

As he explained his situation to me, I could see that his possibilities for success were excellent. I quickly recognized, however, as did he, that the demands on his time might be severe, and that the result could be an unacceptable level of strain on his family. We discussed this part of the problem, and it became apparent that he had given it much prayerful consideration.

After about twenty minutes of discussion this young man carefully worded his petition for help by saying, "Now, I'm not asking you to tell me what I should do, but I am asking for any advice you can give me."

We had known each other for several years, and he wasn't surprised when I asked, "What has the Lord instructed you to do?"

His response was, "I've prayed about it day after day and want to do the Lord's will, but I just can't get an answer. I don't know if he isn't speaking or if I'm just not listening, but I need help. That's why I decided to come and speak with you."

I knew this young man well and knew that he was sincere in his desire to do the Lord's will. I knew also that he had had many spiritual experiences during his life. He was married in the temple. He was a good husband and a fine father. He held daily family and private prayer. Now, faced with an important decision, he came to me because he couldn't get an answer to his prayers.

We discussed the principle of prayer. He explained that he knew that he had been blessed many times with answers to prayers. He said that his wife was once healed through the power of faith and prayer, and he described other times when he had received similar blessings. He even told of times when he had received overpowering promptings, almost as a voice from heaven, guiding him in what he should do. However, he said that he frequently experienced difficulty with a decision where he had a strong desire for a specific outcome. He expressed concern that perhaps he was talking himself into a particular decision rather than truly listening to what God had to say.

I asked him to describe his prayers to me and to discuss the experiences he and his wife had had in prayer. He said that they had explained to Father in Heaven two career options they were considering. They had presented both of these options in an effort to keep their minds totally open to whatever option God may have wanted them to follow. He further explained that they had then asked, "What is the right thing for us to do?" They had expressed a strong willingness to do whatever the Lord chose, but no answer came.

The Lord's Way

I took out my scriptures and we reviewed the instructions Christ provided for Oliver Cowdery regarding prayer. Let's review these instructions here, remembering that even though this counsel was directed specifically to Oliver Cowdery, it serves as a general format for prayer for all of us.

> Behold, you have not understood; you have supposed that I would give it unto you, when you took no thought save it was to ask me.
> But, behold, I say unto you, that you must study it out in your mind; then you must ask me if it be right, and if it is right I will cause that your bosom shall burn within you; therefore, you shall feel that it is right.
> But if it be not right you shall have no such feelings, but you shall have a stupor of thought that shall cause you to forget the thing which is wrong. (D&C 9:7-9.)

We discussed the scripture; I pointed out that Christ instructed us to "study it out" in our own minds, to make a decision and then to "ask . . . if it be right." We were told to decide what we think is right and then to tell God what we think the right choice is. We are then supposed to ask, "Is the decision correct?"

I repeated back to this young man what he had been saying in his prayers: "What is the right thing for us to do?" He quickly realized that he and his wife had never made a decision. He could see that by offering God two options and then asking which one was correct, they had failed to follow God's basic instruction about prayer. They had failed to make a decision.

After we discussed the decision-making process, this young man became quite encouraged. Later, he and his wife approached the Lord once again, only this time with a specific decision, asking if it was right. This time the answer came and the answer was sure. No question or doubt remained in their minds, and they are now successfully promoting their own business with an assurance that they have the approval of the Lord.

Two Types of Prayer

Similar difficulties have been experienced by many of us who have sought to learn God's will in our behalf. We fail to make a decision. We ask the Lord to make the decision for us and to tell us what to do. But, sometimes we feel that we have no sound basis for making a decision. Sometimes we feel a need for inspiration and guidance. This was brought vividly to my attention through the following experience.

A young couple, Larry and Arlene, were speaking with me. They were the parents of two young children. Arlene had had serious health problems in the birth of both children, and she was counseled by her doctor to have no more children as she would likely experience severe complications. Larry and his wife had discussed the matter extensively with their Father in Heaven, and they were seeking to know his will in their behalf.

They were intent on doing God's will and knew that, in general, we are counseled and expected to bring as many children as possible into our homes. They wanted more children. They hoped that God would provide them with an assurance of health and safety if they increased the size of their family in spite of their doctor's warning.

As I spoke with Larry and his wife, I asked them to describe the experiences they had had in speaking with their Father in Heaven. They explained that they had asked "again and again for God to inspire us to know what to do." They indicated that many weeks had gone by, but they had received no answer.

Larry and Arlene had been diligent in petitioning God for assistance, and their faith was strong. They were willing to accept any answer, but they felt no answer had come.

I reviewed with them the Lord's instructions to Oliver Cowdery regarding the proper manner for prayer. (D&C 9:7-9.) Larry was familiar with this passage of scripture, and he quickly said, "Yes, bishop, we know we're supposed to study it out and make a decision and then pray to see if the decision is right, but in this case we have no basis for making a decision. We don't know what to study. We need inspiration from God to tell us what to do. There is no book that will tell us if Arlene will be protected during another pregnancy and birth. Isn't there a valid use of prayer in seeking God's inspiration rather than merely praying for his confirmation of a decision?"

His question showed wisdom. It caused me to stop and ponder, for in a few simple words he clearly identified a need for two very different forms of prayer. One form is a petition to the Lord for wisdom, safety, health, or any other blessings. We aren't necessarily asking him to make a decision for us. We are merely petitioning him for assistance. I call this the "petition prayer."

The second form of prayer is that described by the Lord in his instructions to Oliver Cowdery. It is the prayer we use after we have made a decision and we are trying to determine if our decision is in accordance with God's will. I refer to this as the "decision prayer."

Petition Prayers

Most of the prayers we offer are petition prayers. Before we retire at night we ask the Lord for safekeeping and for a peaceful rest. As parents we petition him

for wisdom in teaching our children. We petition him
for daily inspiration and strength as we face the temp-
tations of Satan. We ask for his assistance as we work,
that we might be efficient and that we might have a
clear mind. We ask for help and guidance in all that we
do.

Within all petition prayers are great opportunities
for expressing gratitude. We should never cease to be
grateful and should always be careful to express fully
our deep gratitude for all our blessings. As we look at
our lives, we see that all we have comes from our
Father in Heaven, and we recognize these blessings in
our humble prayers.

Petition prayers, then, are prayers in which we acknowledge God's hand in all that is good and ask him
for the blessings that we need.

Decision Prayers

We offer decision prayers when we have made a
decision and desire God's confirmation that it is correct. Certainly, in a decision prayer we also express
gratitude to our Father in Heaven for blessings, and
we may even petition him for specific assistance. It's
not likely that a decision prayer would be void of these
elements common to petition prayers. But a decision
prayer is different from a petition prayer in a specific
way. In a decision prayer we don't ask the Lord to help
us make a decision. We tell him of a decision we have
already made and ask if it is right.

A typical question might be phrased something like
this: "Father, it is extremely important that I do the
right thing in proposing marriage to my sweetheart. I
have been praying for guidance and inspiration since I
first started dating her, and our relationship seems to
be proper and good. I love her with all my heart. She
has the same high standards I have, and I'm certain we
can be happy together. I have made the decision to
propose marriage to her this evening. Is this the right

thing for me to do?" A decision prayer will almost always include the general phrase, "I have made this decision. Is it right?"

Make a Decision—Even If It's Wrong

Larry and Arlene had never made a decision. They had been using petition prayers and were still uncertain as to what the correct decision was. However, they were particularly concerned because they had no basis for a decision other than their desire to have more children and the general counsel of the Lord that we should have as many children as we can. They felt unable to make a decision, so they were unable to go to the next step of using a decision prayer.

I asked Larry if they felt inclined one way or the other in their decision. They did. They thought they probably should go ahead and have children. I asked if they had approached God and told him that they felt this way, asking for confirmation that it was right. They had not.

We discussed the two forms of prayer. I pointed out to Larry that God didn't give an unconditional promise for a spiritual manifestation as a result of a petition prayer. He did, however, promise that we would receive a spiritual manifestation in response to a decision prayer. Therefore, we find it necessary to convert our requests for help to decisions. It is necessary to make a decision, even if it's wrong.

God is patient, and if we make a wrong choice and offer it to him in prayer, he will not reject our efforts. In fact, he will give us a "stupor of thought" to indicate that it is wrong. This is a direct answer to our prayer, and we have lost nothing. Rather, we have gained much in that we have eliminated one option in our decision-making.

Larry and Arlene had already made a tentative decision. They left my office and within a short time received the spiritual manifestation they were seeking.

They proceeded with their decision with full confidence that it was right. They are now the proud parents of two more beautiful children, and Arlene is in excellent health. They received an answer after they made a decision and used the correct form of prayer to obtain confirmation that the decision was right.

Five Steps to an Answer

Larry and Arlene's situation is certainly not unique. A young father, Bill, came to me with a similar question. He was worried about the emotional strength of his wife and was not certain that she could handle the pressures and difficulties of another pregnancy and child. They had four young children and felt that maybe they should wait a few years before having more.

Bill described their efforts to receive an answer to their prayers. They had been praying diligently for quite some time and had, as he put it, "received no burning." His choice of words showed that he was aware of the decision prayer described in the Doctrine and Covenants, but he hadn't succeeded in making it work.

I asked Bill to tell me the words they had used in their prayers. He said, "We've been asking God to please tell us whether it's right or wrong for us to put off having another child."

I said, "The answer is *yes!*"

He studied my face to see if he could tell what I was trying to say. I then quickly added, "Yes, it is either right or it is wrong."

I was doing more than playing word games with Bill. I was trying to help him see that even if the Lord had given them a "burning," it wouldn't have told them anymore than my yes did.

Bill said, "Bishop, your answer is much different than the Lord's would be. I can't help but feel that if the Lord gave us a "burning" to tell us yes in answer to our prayer, he would help us to understand what the yes meant."

I agreed wholeheartedly. I told Bill that if the Lord responded to that type of prayer, he would have to do it so the person would know what the answer meant. However, I emphasized that the Lord never promised to answer that type of prayer. He told us to make a decision and then ask if it is right. We can then be sure he will answer because we are following the pattern outlined in the Doctrine and Covenants. I like to think of five steps in obtaining an answer to prayer:

1. Ask the Lord for assistance through petition prayers.
2. Study the issue out in your mind.
3. Make a decision.
4. Pray, requesting confirmation of your decision.
5. Receive a positive response (or go back to step one if the response is negative.)

Let's review each of the five steps in more detail.

Step one: Ask the Lord for assistance through petition prayers. As we face a new decision or problem, we should approach the Lord in full humility and indicate that we want to do the right thing and that we need his help and inspiration in making the decision. We promise dedication in living his commandments in order to be worthy of this inspiration and guidance.

We don't necessarily ask for or expect a "burning" at this point because we haven't yet made any decisions requiring confirmation. Perhaps we will feel a warm, comforting feeling in response to this petition prayer, and we might even be blessed with an understanding or idea that seems to be what we need. God may give revelation in response to this petition prayer. But the promise in the Doctrine and Covenants doesn't guarantee anything so dramatic in response to this initial prayer. Instead, we are encouraged to go on to step two.

Step two: Study the issue out in your mind. This second

step is extremely important. We should think, study, and seek counsel from Church leaders and others until we can make a decision.

During this step we study the scriptures. We read books by Church authorities and others about our topic of concern. We visit our meetinghouse library and use the Church Periodical Index to find articles in Church magazines. We counsel with our fathers (no matter what our age). We discuss the matter with all family members affected by and old enough to participate in the decision.

Perhaps most important, we meditate. We think and analyze. We consider our eternal goals and relate the decision to be made to them.

This second step is not isolated from step number one. We should pray *and* study until we make our decision.

Step three: Make a decision. As simple as it seems, this is the step most often omitted. Often we pray and study and then magically expect a "burning" without making a decision. Or we make a tentative decision but are hesitant to approach the Lord with our decision because we aren't certain it is correct. Strange, isn't it! We want to know if it's right but we're hesitant to ask because we aren't sure. If we were sure, we wouldn't need to ask!

Certainly God recognizes our limited ability to ascertain truth without his inspiration. We should take our tentative decision to the Lord for his confirming vote. He didn't say he would chastise us if it were wrong. He merely said he would tell us it *was* wrong so we could avoid making a mistake, so we could better determine what is right.

Step four: Pray for confirmation of the decision. It is at this point that we finally approach the Lord, firm in our expectation that we shall receive an answer to our prayer. He has promised that we shall receive a burning in our bosom or a stupor of thought. We approach the Lord with a statement like one of the following: "We feel we should have another child now. Is this right?" "I've decided to accept this new job. Is this the right thing for me to do?" "We feel we should encourage John to attend trade school. Are we right?" "Mike may propose to me tonight. I feel good about marrying him and I've decided to say yes. Is this the right thing to do?"

Step five: Receive a positive response from God. All our efforts culminate in this final step. If we receive a burning in the bosom, our task is complete. However, if we receive a stupor of thought, indicating that our decision is not correct, it becomes necessary to begin again at step one. We should go through the first four steps, with a new decision each time, until we receive the burning in our bosom.

Now let's return to Bill and his difficult decision. He was worried about having more children right away because of the emotional strain on his wife.

Bill and I discussed the five steps for obtaining an answer to prayer. He and his wife had never completed step number three, make a decision. After our discussion, he left my office and eventually received the answer he was seeking. In discussing it with him later, I learned that he and his wife decided it would be best to wait before having additional children. They then approached the Lord with this decision and asked for confirmation that it was correct. They received an answer in the form of a stupor of thought and recognized the answer without difficulty.

They then went back to step one. After prayer and discussion, they reached the decision that if the Lord wanted them to have more children right away then they were completely willing to do so. They decided it was right to go ahead and have another child. They went to step four and requested confirmation of this decision. Their prayer was answered with a powerful spiritual manifestation, and they had no further doubt as to what the Lord's will was. They have been happy with their decision ever since.

We must use decision prayers as well as petition prayers. This will help solve many of the problems we experience in determining the will of God.

4

How Do I Ask?

The most eloquent orator could never approach the ability of God to effectively communicate. Certainly, God, in his infinite capabilities, could communicate his desire and will to mankind through powerful and dynamic methods, leaving little doubt in the hearts of those receiving his message as to what his will is.

We only need to think of the experiences of Saul, who was "breathing out threatenings and slaughter against the disciples of the Lord." (Acts 9:1.) On his way to Damascus, accompanied by several associates, Saul received a direct communication from God. He fell to the earth and heard the voice of the resurrected Jesus Christ saying, "Saul, Saul, why persecutest thou me?" (Acts 9:4.) Saul was struck blind for three days until Ananias was commanded by Christ to go and restore his sight. He did, and Saul was baptized. Saul became known as Paul and became a mighty emissary for the Lord.

The communication Saul received from Christ was

effective, and it is only one example of many powerful communications from God to his children. Why then, with our Father in Heaven so capable in the art of communication, do we experience difficulty receiving his communication?

God's Promises Are Limited

Although God's abilities to effectively communicate seem to be without limit, he may not use the same powerful methods with us that he did with Paul. In fact, the scriptures offer a promise based upon the wise condition that we carry the major responsibility for effective divine communication.

When the Lord instructed Oliver Cowdery in the proper manner of prayer, he didn't promise loud thundering or a voice from heaven. He promised a confirming warmth or a negating stupor of thought. He didn't promise an eloquent sermon. He promised a simple yes or no. He has instructed us to think our problems through and decide upon our own solutions and then to ask him only to confirm that our decisions are correct.

Twenty Questions

Without desiring to indicate any lack of respect for the sacred nature of prayer, let's turn our thoughts to a game based on a similar principle, Twenty Questions.

In this familiar game, the individual or panel has to determine what or who the predetermined "secret" is. The panel can ask twenty questions of the moderator, each of which must be designed to receive only a yes or no response. The moderator, who knows the answer, participates only by answering the questions. As in prayer, the full burden of responsibility for determining the answer rests on the one asking the questions. His success depends upon asking the right questions.

A clue is given identifying the answer as animal, vegetable, or mineral. The questions then proceed.

The experienced player eliminates large areas of possibility through broad questions.

Suppose the answer were Winston Churchill. The original clue is that the answer is animal. The questioner might ask: (1) Is it human? (yes); (2) Is this person female? (no); (3) Is he living? (no); (4) Was he involved in entertainment or the performing arts? (no); (5) Was he involved in politics? (yes); (6) Was he an American? (no). Questions would then proceed based on the knowledge that the answer is a deceased male political figure in some country other than the United States.

The inexperienced player frequently jumps to a conclusion before gathering enough information. In the example above, the inexperienced player might ask, "Is it an elephant?" With this approach to questioning, the chances of identifying the answer in twenty questions would be very small.

We can see the importance of asking the right questions. One seeking the answer must ask many general questions. The same is true in prayer. We must ask many questions of ourselves and of God to gain a full understanding of his will. This is reflected in God's instruction to study issues out in our own mind. We must consider all possibilities and gain the broadest understanding before coming to Heavenly Father to ask for divine confirmation. We must avoid asking, with the first clue, "Is it an elephant?"

To Answer Yes or No Is Sometimes Difficult

It is sometimes difficult to answer a question with a yes or a no.

For example, let's consider the answer to be Jack Benny, a famous comedian. Most people know that Jack Benny also played the violin. So, let's imagine the following questions: (1) Is it human? (yes); (2) Is he male? (yes); (3) Is he living? (no); (4) Was he involved in entertainment or the performing arts? (yes); (5) Was he a musician?

Now, how would you answer that last question? True, Jack Benny was a musician, but would it really be fair to the challenger to say yes? He would likely direct the rest of his questions toward identifying a famous musician, and upon failing to do so in twenty questions would probably be disappointed to have been led astray. But, on the other hand, to say, "No, he was not a musician," would be equally wrong—perhaps less misleading, but still wrong.

When we play twenty questions in our family, we diverge from the rules and allow the moderator to qualify his response. For example, he might say, "Yes, he's a musician, but that's not what he's best known for." That usually solves the problem and avoids misunderstandings.

What about in prayer? Do we ever ask questions that can't be answered yes or no? If so, how does the Lord respond?

Imagine that you are a young person, in love with and anxious to marry your sweetheart. You go to the Lord and say, "Father, I love my sweetheart with all my heart, and I believe we should marry. Am I right?" Suppose that you receive a stupor of thought. You are disappointed, but you resign yourself to the thought that you and your sweetheart should not plan on marriage. But, are you right?

The Lord answers either yes or no, and in this case he certainly didn't say yes. What does the no answer mean? Does it mean, "No, don't marry"? If so, you should be able to confirm this by reversing your question and asking for a burning in the bosom.

Suppose that you go to the Lord again in prayer. This time you say, "I've decided not to marry my sweetheart. Is this the right decision?" You may really become confused if the answer to this question is also a stupor of thought. What is the Lord's will? He said no to both questions.

At this point it becomes essential for you to return

to the important step of studying it out in your mind. You must decide upon some other option.

You give serious thought to the matter, and feel that you should continue dating your sweetheart but postpone the decision of marriage. You then pray, "Father, I do feel a great love for my sweetheart and feel that we should continue dating in order to get to know each other better in anticipation of perhaps marrying one day. Is this right?" You may then feel that great comforting warmth as a manifestation from God that you have made the correct decision. Oh, how important it is to ask the right question!

What Does the Stupor Mean?

In twenty questions, we may feel justified in qualifying our responses when questions aren't easily answered yes or no, but in prayer the Lord requires us to return with a better question. He didn't promise to clarify or explain. He did promise to say yes or no.

The stupor of thought may not always mean no. It may mean we haven't asked the right question. We should pursue the issue with new questions until the affirmative, burning response is received. Only through this response are we able to learn what the will of the Lord really is.

5

Why Am I Afraid?

Nearly all who have approached God in prayer have sometime been afraid of his possible response. Have you ever hesitated to ask God if something was right because it was something you really wanted to do and you were afraid God might not approve? Have you ever had difficulty hearing a no response to a prayer because you didn't want to hear it? Have you ever rationalized an action in spite of not having divine confirmation that it was right, when deep inside you felt it might not be? Fear of God's response frequently results from selfish interests and is occasionally a factor in difficulties we experience in receiving and recognizing God's response to our prayers.

What If He Says No?

Joyce recently graduated from high school, regularly dated a returned missionary, and was trying to decide how to respond to his recent proposal of marriage. Her parents objected to her friend because, in their eyes, he suffered from a general lack of spiritual commitment. She felt that she loved him, but did not want to go against her parent's will. Also, she knew that there was some validity to their concerns, and she certainly wasn't confident that she should agree to the marriage.

As she shared her problem with me, we discussed the principle of prayer and its role in this important decision. She had received excellent spiritual training in her youth, and she fully understood how to receive answers to prayer. She even knew that the burden rested on her to make a decision and ask the right question. Her problem? She feared the response!

Joyce was afraid that the Lord might instruct her to leave her boyfriend and find someone new. She knew that he didn't have quite the depth of spiritual commitment that he should, even though he had been raised with the teachings of the gospel and had served a mission. In her love for him, she was willing to overlook these faults, and she greatly feared the idea of losing him.

Faced with this important decision, Joyce had prayed. She had pleaded for guidance; she had poured out her soul. But, she had not proposed a specific decision to the Lord requesting his confirmation that it was right. She was afraid she might be told not to marry. So, Joyce had gone on using petition prayers instead of decision prayers.

Fear can affect our ability to ask the right questions under many circumstances. For example, a couple may decide they want to purchase a new home, but deep inside they feel that they probably can't afford to and shouldn't do so. They pray intently but avoid proposing a specific decision because they fear the response. Instead, they petition the Lord to "help us to know if we should move or not." They use petition prayers instead of decision prayers.

Often, we don't necessarily avoid prayer, but we do frequently avoid asking a specific question of God. We ask God to allow us to do something instead of asking him if it is the right thing to do.

Do You Avoid Hearing the Answer?

Sometimes we submit a decision to the Lord, but we fail to recognize the answer. We don't recognize the stupor of thought that occurs as a response. For example, the couple desiring to purchase a new home may eventually propose this decision in prayer, requesting confirmation. They may receive a stupor of thought in response. They are disappointed; they want to move into a newer home. They don't want to be told no. So, consciously or subconsciously, they fail to recognize the answer. They keep praying, asking the same question over and over. Eventually they complain, "God won't answer our prayers."

We frequently interpret a stupor of thought as no answer at all. Too frequently, upon receiving a negative response from God, we continue to approach him with the proposal, reoffering it for an extended period of time, hoping for his eventual confirmation or acceptance. Sometimes we actually reach the point of deciding, "God must not really care. He hasn't answered my prayer, so I think I will go ahead and do what I want." All the while, he may have been answering, but we may have failed to hear.

Often we know deep within ourselves what the answer probably is, but we express frustration that we haven't received an answer to our prayers. Being fully honest, we would have to admit that we just haven't asked the right question or that we weren't willing to hear the response. We want to do the Lord's will, but we are reluctant to forgo our selfish desires. We don't ask the right questions or we fail to recognize God's answer because we don't want to be disappointed.

Imagine a Visitation from Christ

In the case of Joyce and her difficult decision, I suggested, "Imagine that you are kneeling in prayer and that Jesus Christ suddenly appears to you and speaks with you. Imagine that he comforts you and tells you that you should not marry the young man you are dating, but that there is someone much better that you will meet and one day marry. Would you find it difficult to give up this boy? Would you find it difficult to accept this answer?"

Needless to say, Joyce said that if Christ were to manifest himself to her and comfort her in this manner, she would have no difficulty accepting the answer.

The Holy Ghost: the Comforter

We have received a promise that "by the power of the Holy Ghost ye may know the truth of all things." (Moroni 10:5.) Christ may not appear personally in response to our prayers, yet we have a promise that the Holy Ghost will provide a personal manifestation. Another name for the Holy Ghost, the Comforter, suggests a comforting influence to be felt by all who seek the Lord's guidance. God will not only provide the answers we seek, but will, based on our sincerity, provide the comfort we need to be able to accept the answers.

Through the power of the Holy Ghost, God will answer our prayers in such a manner that we can *know* that we are receiving a manifestation of God's will. The certainty we can have that God has answered our prayers can be as great as if Christ himself were to appear to us. We can be blessed with a feeling of peace and comfort that will make it easy to accept God's will.

What Is There to Fear?

We shouldn't fear to approach the Lord in prayer, for frequently we will find that his will coincides with ours, in spite of our fears to the contrary. God may support our decisions in spite of our fears, but if we are afraid to ask, we will never find out.

Fear of an answer, then, is a tool of Satan to get us to delay asking our questions. We need not fear the response of the Lord, for either we will be pleasantly surprised and find that our fear was unfounded, or we will receive the comforting influence of the Holy Ghost, giving us the comfort and courage that we need to seek something better in patience and faith.

6

What Will I Hear?

I have met and counseled with many people who feel they are performing all the necessary steps to receive God's confirmation of a decision they have made, but they don't know what it feels like to have a "burning" or a "stupor of thought." They fear that they won't recognize the answer when it comes.

Some who have had only infrequent success in hearing God's answers believe that the only way to experience a burning in the bosom is to have an overwhelming, dynamic, spiritual manifestation, comparable, perhaps, to a vision or at least an almost audible voice from heaven. I believe the Lord does, on occasion, answer prayers with this type of spiritual manifestation. But I feel that his response to most of our prayers will be a more subtle communication, a calm or a peaceful feeling.

Make It Burn Really Hot
I had been counseling with Dennis for several weeks. He and his wife had four small children, and he

29

had been having some employment difficulties. Dennis had been looking for a job locally but hadn't been able to find one, so he was thinking about moving to a nearby city, hoping to find a job there.

As Dennis considered the pros and cons associated with the move, he realized that the job market in the city was in a slump. He had no money to make the move, and his wife had deep concerns about pulling up roots and leaving friends.

Although Dennis hadn't succeeded in obtaining a job in recent weeks, the local job market was actually quite good. Dennis, however, being somewhat un-settled by nature, kept wondering if perhaps they should move. He wanted to know if it was God's will that he stay where he was, and he wanted some assur-ance that he would be able to obtain employment locally. He committed himself to obtaining confirma-tion through prayer.

Later, I met with Dennis, and he related his expe-riences of the past few days. He and his wife had ap-proached the Lord with the decision that they would stay in the area and continue to look for work locally. They offered this prayer each day for several days. His wife had experienced a warm, peaceful feeling and a conviction that the decision was right. But he wasn't sure he had received the answer. He wasn't sure he had felt a "burning."

After some discussion, he asked me if we might kneel together in prayer. We did. His prayer was sin-cere. He prayed for several minutes relating the con-siderations affecting the decision. I began to feel warm and peaceful. He spoke of his decision to remain local-ly and asked for confirmation that it was right. He said, "If this decision is right, then please tell me so by giving me a burning in the bosom. And Father, please make it burn *really hot* so I'll recognize it."

After the prayer, I asked Dennis to describe his feelings. He said he wasn't afraid of staying in the area. He even expressed confidence that he could get a job.

He said the idea of moving was based mainly on the excitement of a possible change. In spite of these good feelings, however, Dennis emphasized that he still did not know for sure that God had answered his prayer. He didn't feel a powerful burning sensation. He felt good, but there was no "burning."

My feeling was that Dennis was already receiving the answer. God had been trying for days to tell him the decision was right. Dennis felt good about the decision, but thought he was supposed to have some dynamic spiritual manifestation, something much greater than the simple peace and warmth that he felt. After further discussion with Dennis, he began to recognize that this may have been the case. He realized that he had been waiting for a sign, an unusual manifestation, a mighty voice.

Dennis went home and, with his wife, approached the Lord again. This time he "listened" for the warm, peaceful promptings of the Holy Ghost. He and his wife received those promptings and felt comfortable with their decision.

Speak a Little Louder, Lord

I have thought back to my experience with Dennis many times. I have remembered often his plea that the Lord "make it burn *really hot.*" It was like saying, "Speak louder, God; I can't hear you."

How often do we find ourselves wondering why the Lord won't answer louder? How often, when we fail to hear God's response to our prayers, do we decide that he merely chose not to answer? Sometimes we think God isn't answering because of something we did or didn't do. We never stop to think that he may have been answering the whole time, and we have merely failed to hear his response.

We might compare ourselves to a teenage girl who is in the basement listening to her favorite tapes. The volume is loud. She suddenly decides she wants to ask her mother a question. She turns toward the stairs and yells, confident that her voice will carry upstairs to her mother. She yells, "*Mom? . . . Mom?*" She hears no answer, so she walks to the stairs and yells, quite a bit louder, "*Mother!*" Still no answer, so she reluctantly decides to go upstairs.

Her mother, who has heard her daughter yelling from downstairs, has each time responded in a very calm voice, "Yes, dear?" Each time, she knew she wasn't being heard, but she wanted to teach her daughter an important lesson.

The girl comes running upstairs, finds her mother, and says, "Mom, didn't you hear me calling you?"

The wise mother responds in a gentle voice, "Yes dear, I did."

"Well, why didn't you answer me then?"

"I did, dear; each time you called I answered. You must not have heard me."

"Why didn't you speak louder so I could have heard you?"

"Why didn't you listen harder?" asks the mother. "I spoke as loudly as I should ever need to speak to be heard."

When Dennis said in his prayer, "make it burn *really hot,*" he was saying, "Speak louder." I suspect our Father, in his infinite wisdom, is saying, "Try harder to listen. I am speaking as loudly as I should ever need to speak to be heard."

What Is the "Burning"?

I am aware of a man who, in his youth, was deeply in love and was prepared to propose marriage to his girl friend, but wanted to know that it was right. He prayed daily. He felt so good about the idea of marrying this girl that he would almost bubble over with excitement as he prayed. He felt that an answer never came, yet he continued to feel excited about the idea. He felt the same way before and after his prayers, but he didn't feel anything unusual or special beyond this excitement.

He finally decided to propose marriage in spite of the fact that he felt no answer had come. He just couldn't believe that he might be wrong. In fact, he had erroneously concluded that perhaps the Lord leaves us alone to make our own decisions on such issues. He had decided that since he couldn't get an answer from God, he would have to go ahead with personal faith and confidence that it would work out well.

He was fortunate! They were married and have had many years of happiness. Several years passed before he ever realized that the Lord *had* answered his prayers, over and over, during the time of his decision regarding marriage. As he gained experience in prayer and receiving divine communication, he realized that the feelings of excitement and joy during his prayers were caused by the warmth and peace God had offered as an indication that his decision was correct.

Answers from God can range from silent to audible voices, or from soft feelings to overwhelming spiritual manifestations. I am certain that in response to many prayers the "burning" is an overwhelming, powerful feeling, and that's a wonderful and special blessing. However, in our regular, daily prayers we should anticipate just what this young man felt. We should expect a warm, peaceful feeling inside. This feeling is the burning in the bosom.

What Is the Stupor of Thought?

If we are close to our Father in Heaven and are spiritually in tune, we can approach him in prayer, asking for confirmation concerning a decision we have made. If we feel a warm, peaceful feeling about our decision before, during, and after the prayer, then we have probably received a manifestation that our decision is correct. In answer to those who ask what the stupor of thought feels like, I frequently respond that it is merely a lack of a burning. If you continue to wonder or doubt, or if you have concerns or reservations, you are probably experiencing a stupor of thought.

As oversimplified as it may seem to some, I believe it is truly as simple as that. Remember that "if it be not right you shall have no such feelings, but you shall have a stupor of thought that shall cause you to forget the thing which is wrong." (D&C 9:9.) Forget the thing which is wrong? Stupor of thought? Those are totally different from feelings experienced by the young man trying to gain confirmation that he should propose marriage. He couldn't forget. He was excited. He felt warm and peaceful. But a lack of these warm, peaceful feelings combined with doubt or confusion would have been a stupor of thought. A stupor of thought indicates that our proposal is incorrect and that we need to pursue another option.

How Do I Listen Harder?

The burden is on us to listen harder as we pray. It is our responsibility to recognize the burning or the stupor of thought.

When we pray, do we consciously stop and listen for divine communication to our spirits? A major reason for failing to recognize an answer is that we never listen for it. We must listen spiritually.

Many prayers are beautiful monologues. We often say, "Give me a burning to know if it's right," and then we immediately close our prayer, stand up, and say, "I don't feel a thing!" We must listen! We should think of prayer as a dialogue, a conversation. When we ask a question, we should pause and wait for an answer.

I suggest the following sequence of events within a prayer. We explain our decision and ask for confirmation that it is correct. Then we pause, meditate, feel, listen spiritually. If we feel good and warm inside, we repeat back to the Lord specifically what we think we've been told. We ask for a final confirmation. We pause and listen. Upon continuing to feel a warm peaceful feeling, we close our prayer with gratitude for the response given.

Get in Tune

Often, we try to communicate with our Father in Heaven, but we feel that we are just "out of tune." We feel that listening isn't really the solution, that we have some barrier to our prayers.

I remember seeing an exhibit on sound with a friend of mine. The exhibit consisted of electronic equipment that produced a tone starting at a very low pitch and then steadily increasing to higher and higher frequencies until it went beyond the ability of the human ear to hear.

As we listened to this tone, we compared our hearing ability. At a certain frequency my friend said, "There, it's gone. I don't hear anything anymore." I was amazed. I still heard a shrill squeal very distinctly, and I couldn't conceive that he couldn't hear it. It was loud and piercing. Then, at a slightly higher frequency, I too was unable to hear the tone.

I was fascinated that I was able to hear something he couldn't. He was mildly concerned that he couldn't hear something I could. But most interesting was that just because we couldn't hear sounds at the higher frequencies didn't mean the sounds weren't there. They were, loud and distinct for those whose ears were tuned to hear those frequencies. Volume made no difference. Being in tune made all the difference.

The same is true of radio waves, which are around us everyday. With a good radio, we can tune in whatever it is we want to hear, yet without the tuning mechanism we wouldn't even know the radio waves are there.

We also have a spiritual tuning mechanism. The principles upon which it works are the first four principles and ordinances of the gospel. If we find we are out of tune, we must put things in order so that we can once again feel the closeness of our Father in Heaven.

7

Praying in Spite of Weakness

During the Sermon on the Mount our Savior taught, "Be ye therefore perfect, even as your Father which is in heaven is perfect." (Matthew 5:48.) Although this teaching is available to Christians the world over, only those who have the restored gospel of Jesus Christ fully comprehend the meaning of this great challenge. We have been taught that we can attain godhood. However, how close to this perfection must we be to be worthy of receiving answers to our prayers?

Just How Worthy?

I remember a young mother of two small children. Her husband, totally inactive in the Church, had imposed severe restrictions on her religious involvement. She was not able to attend Church nor hold a Church assignment. She was not able to receive visits from home teachers or make financial contributions to the Church. She occasionally found herself in unrighteous surroundings due to her efforts to appease her husband's wishes. In spite of her problems, she made a significant effort to make a success of her marriage.

Eventually her husband left her; their marriage ended in divorce. She was left with the two children to raise. She had no means of providing an income. She received no assistance from her former husband. She was in despair and felt that the whole world had come in on top of her.

I counseled with this good sister, and she was comforted as she saw the material aid that was available through the Church. But, her greatest need was spiritual. She found herself facing many decisions and needed help from God to know how to make those decisions.

We discussed prayer and the important role it should play in her life. I learned that she hadn't prayed for years. I asked why. She explained that she hadn't felt worthy. She felt that God would not be willing to hear her prayers because of her sins.

Freed from the unreasonable limitations that had been imposed by her husband, she was now able to attend her meetings and hold family prayers and family home evenings. She was able to live much closer to the teachings of the gospel and repented of her transgressions. She developed a strong feeling of self-worth and learned to pray openly and fervently.

As I think over the many tragic experiences in this young sister's life, I believe the most tragic might have been her mistaken feeling that she was not worthy to pray. This single, self-imposed restriction influenced her relationship with her Father in Heaven far more than the restrictions imposed by her husband. The Lord would have listened to her prayers. She was not unworthy to pray. The most severe restriction in her life she had imposed upon herself unnecessarily.

A Prodigal Son

That the Lord is willing to listen to those who are unworthy has been demonstrated to me many times.

While serving as a bishop, I occasionally had the special experience of seeing a prodigal son or daughter return to the fold. I remember one young man in particular. I had known him since his early teens, and I shared much of his parents' agony when, at about the age of seventeen, he adopted the ways of the world. He spent about three years living a life totally apart from the gospel. It would be difficult to overstate the depth and severity of his transgressions.

One day he felt an overwhelming sense of urgency to get his life in order. He fell to his knees in the privacy of his room and had a heart rending, spiritual experience with his Father in Heaven. Later, he met with me and poured out his soul, asking for help in resolving his problems. We prayed together, and both of us felt a mighty spirit present with us. We knew that God was there, ready and anxious to help.

In spite of this young man's unworthiness, God answered his prayers. The desire he had to repent and change his life is the thing that made the difference. He hadn't, at the time of his first meeting with me, made a lot of changes in his life, but he had a desire to do so. In fact, it took many months of dedicated effort before he finally overcame some of the bad habits he had developed over the years, but he had no difficulty communicating with God in spite of those problems. God was patient with this young man. God knew he wanted to change and that it would be difficult for him to change everything at once.

But What about the Higher Laws?

Somehow it doesn't seem difficult for most people to accept the fact that God is willing to be patient as the repentant sinner gradually overcomes major transgressions. Yet, the same person who finds no difficulty accepting this fact may be suffering seriously from feelings of unworthiness, even though he has not transgressed major laws.

I remember a young mother who felt such a high

level of self-condemnation that she avoided prayer, and when she did pray, her prayers were hollow. She didn't feel worthy, and therefore her prayers lacked confidence and faith.

In discussions with her, I learned that she felt guilty about her lack of effectiveness as a mother. She wasn't as patient with her children as she felt she should be, and she occasionally lost her temper. She was disappointed in herself for not being a more effective missionary or a more ardent genealogist. These problems, minor in comparison to those of the prodigal son considered earlier, racked her soul and caused her to feel she wasn't worthy to communicate with God. Certainly with the prodigal son, who was trying to live the basic commandments, God was patient. Wouldn't he be that much more patient with this mother who was striving to live these higher laws?

Christ's comforting counsel to us is "Ask, and it shall be given you; seek, and ye shall find; knock, and it shall be opened unto you: For every one that asketh receiveth." (Matthew 7:7-8.) He didn't attach any conditions of special worthiness. We teach people the world over to pray, with a promise that "by the power of the Holy Ghost ye may know the truth of all things." (Moroni 10:5.)

The Evil Spirit Teacheth Not a Man to Pray

Why do we allow ourselves to believe we are not worthy to receive God's inspiration and guidance? We have been told that "the evil spirit teacheth not a man to pray, but teacheth him that he must not pray." (2 Nephi 32:8.) It is my firm belief that Satan uses our feelings of guilt to make us feel unworthy to pray. I believe he makes us think, "Surely God won't listen to me. I'm not worthy."

When we feel that we are unworthy to pray, we should remember that it is Satan, not God, who wants us to have those feelings. Then we may not sacrifice the precious opportunity of divine communication.

I recall a young man who was making repeated efforts to overcome a bad habit. Frequently, he would vow to himself that he would never do it again. Then, whenever he did it again, he would feel so guilty that he would avoid prayer for a time. He was a fine young man, and I challenged him, "Don't you believe that God knows how difficult this problem is for you? Don't you believe that he is anxious to hear from you even after a failure? Perhaps that is when he wants most to hear from you!"

If we have transgressed, but we avoid prayer, Satan has us right where he wants us. God wants us to pray, especially when we are guilt ridden. But Satan implants within our hearts the feeling that we are not sufficiently worthy to pray.

God does want to hear our prayers in spite of our transgressions. However, it is essential that we communicate with a repentant attitude. Although our repentance may not be complete, we must pray with a broken heart and a contrite spirit. We must be sincere in wanting to make a change in our life. Even if we don't feel capable of changing, as long as we sincerely desire to change we can effectively communicate with God.

8

Developing Self-Mastery

God expects to hear our prayers in spite of our weaknesses. He knows how difficult our mortal existence is, and he expects us to progress a little at a time. "For he will give unto the faithful line upon line, precept upon precept; and I will try you and prove you herewith." (D&C 98:12.)

Will He Be Forever Patient?

Yet many of us feel that we suffer from a seeming lack of progress. Perhaps we are bothered by a bad habit or by the failure to develop a good habit. Maybe we suffer from an inability to live some specific gospel principle. Perhaps we feel unable to control our temper.

What about these deep-seated bad habits and problems that we've unsuccessfully tried to root out for years? Is God going to be patient with us forever? Does he eventually give up on us when we promise for the twentieth time that we will never do it again and for the twentieth time break our promise? Does God really

41

want to hear our prayers when our self-control seems so limited?

Of course, he does want to hear from us, and as we pray we should have no difficulty hearing his response as long as we approach him with a humble, repentant attitude.

A Never-Ending Cycle

Let's consider the case of the young man briefly mentioned in the previous chapter who was attempting to overcome a bad habit. Every time he failed to live up to his promise, he would discontinue his prayers. He felt that he had failed God.

This young man told me what it was like to be on a spiritual low. He would be active in his meetings, and on the surface everything seemed fine, but he would be making little effort to overcome his personal habit because of his discouragement. He would eventually have a positive experience that would cause him to humbly and tearfully approach his Father in Heaven, asking for forgiveness and promising, "I will never do that again!" He was sincere. He was committed, and he believed he would succeed. He felt close to his Father in Heaven and was successful in receiving a feeling of peace and comfort in answer to his prayer. The reason he received an answer wasn't because he had conquered his problem. He received an answer because he was sincere in wanting to repent and improve his life. Eventually, however, Satan seemed to catch and challenge him at a moment of weakness. He would yield, and the cycle would begin all over again. I believe many of us experience this cycle, and I diagram it as shown below.

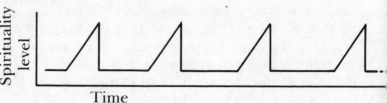

Notice that it is a never-ending cycle that goes no-where. Our level of spirituality climbs, but each time drops back to the same low level we were at previously. No progress is made that isn't completely lost with the next failure.

This is not because we still have a bad habit. It is be-cause we don't think God wants to hear our prayers. Satan wins again.

Notice something else about the diagram. The spacing between successive positive efforts increases. Each time we fail, we delay longer before we try again. Eventually some people quit trying and say, "It's no use; I'll never change." And they don't!

Make a Different Promise

Obviously, the ideal solution is for us to conquer our problems. But, sometimes our habits are deeply ingrained. Sometimes it's a monumental task to root them out. So, what should we do about prayer while we repent? The answer is simple; we should use it as a tool.

Let's go back to the young man's positive decision and commitment. He prays and makes a promise to his Father in Heaven. Now, if he is certain that he will never do it again he should say so. But, in our example he has already tried many times before, and he is not confident enough to make that type of commitment and promise. If this is the case, then he shouldn't make the promise! One reason the young man felt so low was because he broke his promise to "never do it again."

There is a different promise that can be used in a case like this. Actually, it is a set of two promises. The first is, "I promise to make every effort to avoid and resist this temptation!" The second is, "If I ever do transgress in this manner again, I promise to speak to thee concerning it on the very day that it occurs." First, we promise to try hard, and second, we promise that in the event of failure we won't avoid prayer.

The Celestial Cycle

With this approach, it is possible that we will still have a cycle of successes and failures. But, there is a high likelihood that the cycle will be continually lifting us closer and closer to the celestial life we are seeking.

In the earlier cycle, we saw an immediate drop to the previous low level of spirituality. This was mainly due to a cessation of prayer. But, if we keep the second part of our promise to God, that we will, in the same day, approach him in prayer, we will be able to avoid dropping back to that low spiritual level. This is the time to pray harder, more intensely, in an effort to immediately regain the highest possible spiritual level.

I believe that in this prayer of repentance, it is entirely appropriate to say, "Father, I fell again. I tried hard, but it seems so difficult for me. But I am still very willing to try, and I pray for forgiveness and strength and help for the future." We then close our prayer with the same two promises we made earlier, to try again and to pray during the same day we fail, if we happen to fail again.

God is loving. He is understanding. He knows how difficult these things are, and I firmly believe he will be patient as long as he sees a sincere effort on our part.

The pattern that results from this approach to developing self-mastery is diagrammed below. Notice that the spirituality level is increasing. Yes, there are occasional drops, but through continued prayers we are able to recover without ever dropping as low as we were before.

Notice also that the spacing, just as before, is increasing, except in this case the time between failures is increasing instead of the time between successes. At some point in time, we reach a spiritual level high enough to allow us to promise with confidence, "Father, I will never do that again," and we will succeed.

We can't afford to avoid prayer because we have

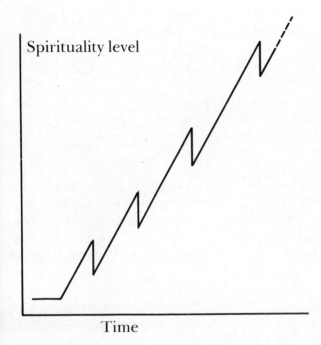

transgressed. Prayer is the tool we need to develop the strength to succeed in spite of our transgressions.

The Hourglass

As I have discussed these principles with certain people, some have said, "But I don't see how I can ever conquer *my* problem; it just seems impossible."

When a person is this discouraged, prayer is essential to provide spiritual strength and hope. A beautiful analogy used by Dr. C. A. Riddle of Brigham Young University, somewhat modified herein, teaches an important lesson about discouragement in trying to overcome difficult problems.

The analogy is based on an hourglass. A person begins his spiritual progression from the bottom of the hourglass. He has full freedom in where he goes and what he does, and he feels comfortable with his life. He feels comfortable being a social drinker, using occasional strong language, golfing on Sunday, and a large variety of other activities. He feels free.

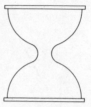

The missionaries knock on our friend's door; let's call him Mike. Mike begins the conversion process. He learns about God and of God's expectations for him. Mike is raised slightly in his level of spirituality. He begins to feel uncomfortable using strong language in the presence of the missionaries. He begins to pray, and as he does, he learns that he doesn't feel good about doing some of the other things he is accustomed to doing. He climbs to a higher level in the hourglass. But he has a smaller range of freedom in which he feels comfortable. He feels somewhat restricted, but continues to see the missionaries.

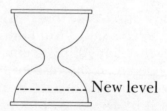

New level

As his conversion continues, Mike learns more and more about his life that he must change. He needs to keep the Sabbath day holy. He must give up alcohol and tobacco. He needs to study the scriptures and feels more of an obligation to give his employer a full day's work. He climbs higher in the hourglass, and his comfort zone gets tighter and tighter.

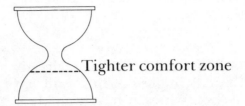

Tighter comfort zone

Mike begins noticing how tight and uncomfortable this new way of life is and feels that his freedom is being threatened. He feels that perhaps this new way of life is unnecessarily restrictive. Then he learns that he is expected to pay a full ten percent of his income to the Church as well as make many other generous financial offerings. He has come close to the narrow neck of the hourglass, but simply gives up saying, "I can't do it; I quit!" He then sinks back to the bottom of the hourglass and resumes his earlier, less-restricted life-style. He breathes a sigh of relief and relaxes in his "more comfortable" surroundings.

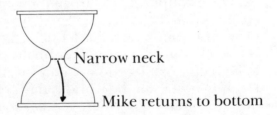

Narrow neck

Mike returns to bottom

What Mike never understood was that his feelings of discomfort were temporary, and that if he had stuck it out he could have burst through the narrow neck of the hourglass and been very comfortable above it. He could have continued to climb in the top half of the hourglass, feeling less and less restricted all the time. He could have become as God, being the freest of all. Instead, he fell back to the bottom where, in the eternities, he will be the most restricted of all, never having the freedom associated with celestial living.

Our Own Narrow Necks

Most of us who have already joined the restored Church of Jesus Christ still have our own "narrow necks." We each have something that just seems impossible to do, and so we sometimes don't even try. We go back down to the bottom of the hourglass with respect to that specific principle. However, if we pick ourselves up after a failure, we are eventually able to burst through the narrow neck and thus fully conquer that specific problem.

Some still say, however, that it's just not worth the effort. They don't feel they could ever be happy or comfortable paying their tithing or doing their genealogical research. They find it impossible to believe they could ever be happy doing something that, right now, seems so restrictive and difficult. There is an important principle that they need to learn: *once we break through the narrow neck, we no longer feel restricted with respect to that principle of the gospel.*

For example, it is nearly impossible for the addicted smoker to believe that someday he might not need or want to smoke. He hasn't passed through the narrow neck. But when a smoker finally conquers his habit, he feels great freedom. Likewise, all but a relatively few individuals in the world today are very content in never commiting murder. We feel no restriction in not being allowed to kill. The same can be true with all principles of the gospel.

We should use prayer as a tool to get through the narrow neck instead of assuming that God doesn't want to hear from us because we are having trouble solving a specific problem.

God is patient. He loves us, and he knows that our progression will be step by step. He won't give up on us if we don't give up on ourselves. Prayer is the key to self-mastery.

9

Learning to Forgive Ourselves

I have known several people who condemned themselves for transgressions that had occurred many years before, even though they felt they had followed all the steps of repentance. Almost always, their self-condemnation inhibited prayer. But in all cases, prayer was needed to help remove the feelings of guilt. Prayer is a magnificent tool to help us forgive ourselves.

The Story of Enos
The story of Enos, from the Book of Mormon, has inspired many people in their prayers. Part of this beautiful story is repeated here:

> Behold, I went to hunt beasts in the forests; and the words which I had often heard my father speak concerning eternal life, and the joy of the saints, sunk deep into my heart.
>
> And my soul hungered; and I kneeled down before my Maker, and I cried unto him in mighty prayer and supplication for mine own soul; and all the day long did I cry unto

him; yea, and when the night came I did still raise my voice high that it reached the heavens.

And there came a voice unto me, saying: Enos, thy sins are forgiven thee, and thou shalt be blessed. (Enos 1:3-5.)

Steps to Repentance

Generally, when we begin to feel, as Enos did, remorse for our transgressions, we begin to repent. We discontinue the sin, pray, and promise never to do it again; when necessary, we confess it to an authority in the Church.

The steps to repentance are sometimes listed as follows:

1. Recognize our action as a transgression.
2. Feel remorse for having transgressed.
3. Resolve never to repeat the sin.
4. Restore what was taken, asking for forgiveness.
5. Confess our transgression to the bishop (if the transgression was severe.)
6. Refrain from repeating the sin in the future.

As a result of our repentance, whatever form it takes, we feel some sense of relief and comfort. We feel that our burden has been lightened and that we are closer to our Father in Heaven. We feel more comfortable in prayer and are generally once again able to develop meaningful communication with God.

Sometimes, however, we continue, perhaps for years, to feel some discomfort and guilt. Frequently this is the case if the transgression was extremely serious. We feel that perhaps God hasn't forgiven us, even though our bishop exercised his judgment in the matter. We wonder if perhaps we held back a little when we spoke with the bishop; we sometimes wonder if perhaps the bishop made a mistake. We continue to feel guilty in spite of what was intended to be complete and total repentance. We feel that God probably has not forgiven us, and we certainly haven't forgiven ourselves.

A fine middle-aged sister came to me with deep remorse for a sin she had committed fifteen years earlier. She had discussed it with her bishop at that time, and he had exercised his responsibility and judged that her repentance was adequate. Although the transgression was serious, he assured her that her fellowship in the Church was to remain intact and that she should make every effort to forget about the sin. He told her "not to worry about it anymore." He assured her that she had taken the necessary steps to obtain forgiveness.

I had no reason to question the judgment and inspiration of that bishop. I believe he was right. I believe he exercised the right judgment. Why, then, did this woman continue to feel guilty? Why hadn't she felt the cleansing influence of her baptism and received peace and comfort from the Holy Ghost?

The Repentance Process—All the Steps

I am sure that each situation is different, and that there might be as many answers to these questions as there are situations. However, one possible answer is that some repentance steps might have been bypassed. Here is a more complete list of the steps to repentance:

1. Recognize our act as a transgression.
2. Have remorse for having transgressed and have a heartfelt desire to receive forgiveness.
3. Resolve never to repeat the sin again.
4. Confess our sin to our Father in Heaven. Request his help in repentance and promise to take whatever steps are required to obtain forgiveness.
5. Confess our sin to the individual or group that we offended and request their forgiveness.
6. Restore whatever was taken or damaged.
7. Confess to our bishop, if appropriate. Express to him a willingness to take whatever steps are required to obtain forgiveness.
8. Receive forgiveness from the Church (through the judgment of the bishop), if appropriate. This

can occur with or without a Church court or disciplinary action. The decision is made by the bishop.

9. Pray again to our Father in Heaven. Tell him that forgiveness has been received from the Church and ask for confirmation that repentance is complete. Ask for a manifestation of his forgiveness. Pray each day and allow the Lord his due time to decide when he will forgive.

10. Receive the manifestation of the forgiveness of God the Father. This comes as a burning in the bosom as a result of fervent, patient prayer.

11. We forgive ourselves.

Let's go back to the sister who had transgressed and repented fifteen years earlier, but had been unable to forgive herself. I reviewed with this sister a list of steps similar to the list above. As we reviewed the list, it became apparent that she had never gone beyond step number eight. She had tried to follow her bishop's counsel to forget that it ever happened, but when she was unable to do so, she assumed that she still carried a burden of guilt. She never completed steps nine and ten and thus never received a manifestation of God's forgiveness. The result was that she was never able to forgive herself.

As we discussed the situation, she suddenly recognized the possibility that God had long since forgiven her, but she had never asked to find out if that was the case. She, like so many others, had neglected to ask him; perhaps she had assumed that she could never receive a spiritual manifestation similar to that of Enos. Thus, she never learned of God's possible forgiveness in all those years.

Like unto Enos

After our discussion, she held a special fast to obtain a spiritual manifestation of God's forgiveness. Like Enos, she was assured of God's acceptance of her repentance and of his forgiveness.

As an important step in repentance, we must fully

confess our transgression and ask God's forgiveness. But after the completion of all we know how to do toward repentance, we should approach our Father and say, "I have completed all that I know how to do to repent of my sins. I feel that I am ready for forgiveness. If this is right, please give me a warmth in my soul to know that I am forgiven."

If the burning does not come, if it is not yet time for God to bless us with a manifestation of his forgiveness, then we should ask him what steps are yet necessary. We should ask to know what to do to obtain complete forgiveness. We need to study it out, to find out what it is and do it, even if it is just to be patient for a while longer.

We have the promise that we can receive God's forgiveness. Each of us can have an experience like that of Enos. President Spencer W. Kimball has said we "should go to the Lord in 'mighty prayer' " and never cease our supplications until we "shall, like Enos, receive the assurance that [our] sins have been forgiven by the Lord." However, he emphasized, "It is unthinkable that God absolves serious sins upon a few requests." (*Ensign*, Nov. 1980, p. 98.) We must be patient and diligent. The experience of Enos is available to all of us, and we should not give up until we receive it.

10

Exercising and Building Faith

Probably everyone who has prayed has at some time had some doubt as to whether an answer would be forthcoming. There are even those who pray regularly with an attitude of, "I'm sure I won't get an answer. I never do." This usually becomes a self-fulfilling prophecy. I believe that God is generally unwilling to answer a faithless request, and even if he chooses to answer, I doubt that a faithless person will hear the response.

Many of us, however, have had success with prayer, and prayer is an important tool in our lives. Yet we occasionally encounter a difficult decision and begin to feel some concern that we might not receive the divine guidance we need. Sometimes we hesitate to admit, even to ourselves, that we are having doubts. We are afraid that if we admit that our doubts exist, we will fail.

Prayer as a Tool

The most important tool for strengthening faith is prayer itself. Receiving an answer to a prayer automatically strengthens our faith. If, on one occasion, we pray with some doubt but with a desire to believe, and receive a divine response, our doubts will be lessened the next time we pray.

Consider someone who is just beginning to develop faith. He may have failed to recognize answers on previous occasions and therefore feels that he has never received an answer to a prayer. How can he build his faith?

The scriptures are full of promises that anything we ask in righteousness, with faith, we shall receive. This magnificent promise of the Book of Mormon is one of the best known:

> And when ye shall receive these things, I would exhort you that ye would ask God, the Eternal Father, in the name of Christ, if these things are not true; and if ye shall ask with a sincere heart, with real intent, having faith in Christ, he will manifest the truth of it unto you, by the power of the Holy Ghost.
>
> And by the power of the Holy Ghost ye may know the truth of all things. (Moroni 10:4-5.)

The promise is absolute. If we but ask with faith and real intent, we can learn the truth of all things by the power of the Holy Ghost.

Certainly a manifestation from the Holy Ghost would promote faith. Therefore, if we exercise faith and are successful in receiving divine guidance, we receive stronger faith. Simply stated, faith begets faith! To develop a higher level of faith, we must exercise the faith we already have.

Positive Feedback

Faith and the Holy Ghost are both mentioned by Joseph Smith in his statement of the first four principles and ordinances of the gospel:

> We believe that the first principles and ordinances of the Gospel are: first, Faith in the Lord Jesus Christ; second,

Repentance; third, Baptism by immersion for the remission of sins; fourth, Laying on of hands for the gift of the Holy Ghost." (Article of Faith 4.)

As we enter the true Church of Jesus Christ, we receive the right to have the Holy Ghost as an eternal companion, based on our worthiness. Thus, we have the right to continual feedback that in turn tends to strengthen our faith. If we take advantage of this feedback, our faith continually increases.

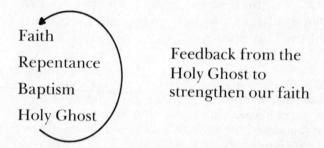

Faith

Repentance

Baptism

Holy Ghost

Feedback from the
Holy Ghost to
strengthen our faith

Let's analyze what we mean by *feedback*. Most of us have been in a room where a public address system is turned up too loud. A high-pitched squeal occurs. The voice of the speaker, or sometimes just the background noise in the room, is picked up by the microphone and amplified through the loudspeakers. If the volume is too high or if the speakers are placed too near the microphone, the microphone picks up this amplified sound and amplifies it again to an even greater volume. The amplified sound is picked up again and again by the microphone, resulting in this high-pitched ringing. This situation can be diagrammed as follows:

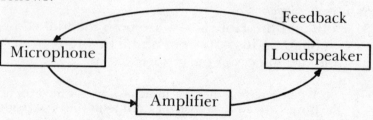

Feedback

Microphone

Loudspeaker

Amplifier

Obviously, in a public address system this feedback is undesirable. It prevents the system from performing its intended purpose.

The solution to the problem of feedback in a public address system is to break the cycle. In order to do this, certain precautions are taken and electronic adjustments are made. For example, the loudspeaker is not placed near the microphone. Also, the electrical gain of the amplifier is adjusted so that feedback does not normally occur. The result is that the cycle is broken, as shown below:

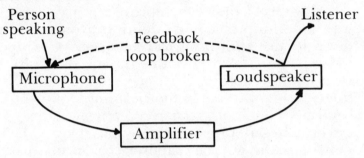

Then the public address system works as it should.

The Spiritual Feedback Loop
This feedback system is similar to a feedback system that should play a part in our lives each day. It can be diagrammed as follows:

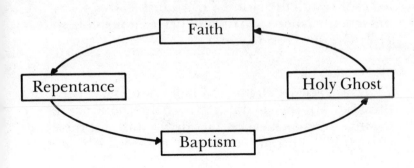

Faith

As our faith grows, we feel motivated to improve our lives. Even in the earliest stages of spiritual progression, the Spirit of Christ (frequently referred to as conscience) prompts us to improve our lives and actions. When we transgress, something tells us it is wrong, and we feel as though we should change. There is a natural tendency to repent. Faith promotes repentance.

Repentance

As we feel a desire to improve our lives, we begin with a specific problem. We decide to avoid telling lies, or we decide to stop using bad language. As we repent, we want our sin to be washed away; we desire the cleansing of baptism. If we have already been baptized, we want to apply the cleansing power of that baptism to the transgression recently overcome. This can be done, after repentance, by partaking of the sacrament. In this way, our baptismal covenant can be renewed.

Baptism

We are baptized not only for past sins, but for all future sins. Repentance allows our baptism, performed years previously, to wash away even recent sins.

As we repent and have our sins cleansed through baptism, we become worthy to receive divine assurances through the Holy Ghost. The fact that we are living a better, more worthy life makes it possible for the Holy Ghost to reside with us.

The Holy Ghost

As we receive divine guidance and assurance from the Holy Ghost, our faith grows, thus completing the positive feedback cycle. The divine promptings from the Holy Ghost increase our faith, which in turn creates an even greater desire to repent. The cycle continues as follows:

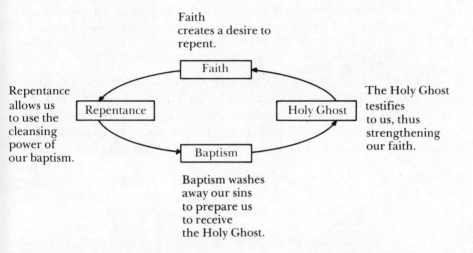

Faith
creates a desire to
repent.

Faith

Repentance
allows us
to use the
cleansing
power of
our baptism.

Repentance

Holy Ghost

The Holy Ghost
testifies
to us, thus
strengthening
our faith.

Baptism

Baptism washes
away our sins
to prepare us
to receive
the Holy Ghost.

As we continue in this cycle, our faith grows, and we come ever closer to the divine perfection that we seek.

To Stop the Feedback—Satan's Goal

The difference between this positive feedback cycle and that of the public address system is that in this system we want the positive feedback. In the public address system, we try to avoid the feedback. We have seen that in the case of the public address system certain steps can be taken to stop the cycle and prevent the feedback.

Our spiritual feedback system can also be broken. We must make every effort to prevent the breaking of the cycle, for Satan is trying to prevent positive feedback from occurring. If he can break the loop at any point, he begins to destroy our faith.

Satan can do this by convincing us that we don't need to repent, that we are beyond forgiveness, or that guilt is merely culturally induced and doesn't really come from God. He tries to convince us that baptism isn't really important, that we don't need to confess our transgressions to our bishop, that the spiritual feelings we have experienced weren't really from the Holy Ghost, or any of dozens of other false ideas. Satan wants to break our cycle and thus destroy our faith.

Promote the Positive Feedback

The way to build faith is to promote this positive feedback. We should have faith in Jesus Christ, repent of our sins, renew our baptismal covenants, and listen to the Holy Ghost. We should allow the faith produced by these things to swell within our bosoms, increasing our faith:

> Now, we will compare the word unto a seed. Now, if ye give place, that a seed may be planted in your heart, behold, if it be a true seed, or a good seed, if ye do not cast it out by your unbelief, that ye will resist the Spirit of the Lord, behold, it will begin to swell within your breasts; and when you feel these swelling motions, ye will begin to say within yourselves—It must needs be that this is a good seed, or that the word is good, for it beginneth to enlarge my soul; yea, it beginneth to enlighten my understanding, yea, it beginneth to be delicious to me. (Alma 32:28.)

As our faith grows and we have more spiritual experiences, we will kneel in prayer with greater confidence that God will hear and answer our prayers. We will grow spiritually until our confidence is no longer based on faith, but on knowledge. For, as Alma tells us, if we will allow the seed to grow within us, we will no longer be reliant on faith:

> And now, behold, is your knowledge perfect? Yea, your knowledge is perfect in that thing, and your faith is dormant; and this because ye know, for ye know that the word hath swelled your souls. (Alma 32:34.)

Our faith will grow daily as we promote this positive feedback.

11

Will We Always Get an Answer?

This book has covered many aspects of how to pray and receive answers to prayer. But even after we are using all the principles of effective prayer, will we always get an answer?

I believe the answer is definitely yes. However, I also believe the question deserves more analysis.

The Book of Mormon promises, "By the power of the Holy Ghost ye may know the truth of all things." (Moroni 10:5.) I believe that promise fully. I believe also, however, that the answer may sometimes be slow in coming. This may be true even when we pray effectively. Many hours, days, weeks, or even years of study and prayer may be required before an answer comes. Yes, an answer will come, but it may take time and require patience.

The Trial of Our Faith

Most of us feel that our problems are urgent. We want answers right now. Patience is sometimes an elusive virtue.

When I become impatient, I think about the story of Enos. Enos prayed all day and continued praying into the night. He had to be patient. He was patient.

Why are we required to exercise patience? Moroni said:

> I would show unto the world that faith is things which are hoped for and not seen; wherefore, dispute not because ye see not, *for ye receive no witness until after the trial of your faith.* (Ether 12:6; italics added.)

This beautiful passage suggests that God, in his infinite wisdom, holds back the spiritual witness in some cases until after we have proven our faith and desire.

Enos passed the trial of his faith. What a different story we would have if he had given up five minutes after starting his prayer, or worse yet, just five minutes before his miraculous communication with God.

God will always answer our prayers, but he may try our faith, and we must pass the trial.

But Some Answers Can't Wait

But what about answers that can't wait? While serving as a bishop, I was faced with many decisions, perhaps fifteen or twenty each week, that had to be made. They couldn't be delayed. Shall we call Sister James to be the Relief Society president? Should I ask Brother Nelson to contribute an additional $500 to the building fund? Shall we provide financial assistance to the Jackson family?

We all face daily decisions that are every bit as important as the examples above. Shall I punish Mark for being home late? Shall we buy a new car? Shall I continue dating Susan?

Since some problems just can't wait, it is important to realize that God will provide the help we need at the time we really need it. If we need to accept or reject an offer of employment by Friday, it's likely he will help us by Friday. If we need immediate inspiration to deal with a crisis with one of our children, he will likely assist us immediately. If we are trying to decide whether or not to sell our home, but there is no urgency, we may not receive his guidance for many weeks or months. We will receive an answer when we truly need it, based on God's wisdom.

12

Passing the Trial of Our Faith

Perhaps the most important factor in effective prayer is the need to approach God with humility, with a sincere purpose and real intent. Almost nothing else matters if this is done.

One danger of a book like this is the tendency to consider prayer as a mechanical process. The danger exists that some will pray with all the suggested methods, but with little or no sincerity.

Although it is important to improve the quality of our prayers, I believe that the Lord will respond even to a clumsy prayer offered by someone with little understanding of how to pray, as long as the prayer is offered humbly and sincerely.

Mormon said:

> For behold, God hath said a man being evil cannot do that which is good; for if he offereth a gift, or prayeth unto God, except he shall do it with real intent it profiteth him nothing.
>
> For behold, it is not counted unto him for righteousness. . . .

And likewise also it is counted evil unto a man, if he shall pray and not with real intent of heart; yea, and it profiteth him nothing, for God receiveth none such. (Moroni 7:6-7, 9.)

It is essential that we pray with real intent for our communications to be effective.

Perform All the Steps

Although our sincerity and intent are more important than all other principles of effective prayer, it is prudent for us to improve the quality of our prayers continually. The following summary may help.

Use Good Prayer Habits

Pray fervently, frequently, and privately. Pray while kneeling. Pray vocally. Fast when appropriate, and as you fast, pray.

Avoid vain repetitions. Don't unthinkingly say the same words you said last night and the night before. Don't allow your mind to wander. Give thanks for the many blessings you have received.

Make a Decision

As you approach the Lord for help in making a decision, remember the difference between petition prayers and decision prayers. Petition the Lord for help. Study the issue out in your own mind and make a decision. Then go to the Lord, using a decision prayer, and ask for his confirmation.

Ask the Right Question

Ask the right question so that God can give you a positive response. If you receive a stupor of thought, return to God with another option. Repeat this process until you receive a burning in the bosom.

Don't Fear the Response

Don't avoid learning the will of God out of fear of

disappointment. The comforting influence of the Holy Ghost can help you accept the will of God. And, God may agree with your desires. You will never know if you don't ask.

Listen Harder

When you find yourself thinking that God isn't answering, the problem may be that you aren't listening. Get closer to God. When you ask a question, listen for an answer. It will come.

Pray in Spite of Weakness

Pray even though you have faults. As long as you are sincerely trying to overcome your faults, the Lord will answer your prayers.

Promote Positive Feedback

Exercise your faith, no matter how weak it may be, to improve your life through repentance. As you do, the Holy Ghost will help you strengthen your faith.

Pass the Trial of Your Faith

Recognize that God will, in his wisdom, bless you with inspiration and help when you truly need it. He may sometimes try your faith beforehand. You must pass that trial.

If we will follow the principles of prayer and sincerely try to improve our communication with God, we will come to know that he hears and answers our prayers, and we will be able to hear those answers when they come.

Index